Contents

Starters to Share

Best Asian-Style Ribs

- **2 full racks baby back pork ribs, split into 3 sections each**
- **6 ounces hoisin sauce**
- **½ cup maraschino cherries, drained**
- **½ cup rice wine vinegar**
- **2 tablespoons minced fresh ginger**
- **4 green onions, chopped (optional)**

1. Combine ribs, hoisin sauce, cherries, vinegar and ginger in **CROCK-POT®** slow cooker. Add enough water to cover ribs.

2. Cover; cook on LOW 6 to 7 hours or on HIGH 3 to 3½ hours. Sprinkle with green onions before serving, if desired.

Makes 6 to 8 servings

Prep Time: 10 to 15 minutes
Cook Time: 6 to 7 hours (LOW) or 3 to 3½ hours (HIGH)

Hot Broccoli Cheese Dip

½ **cup (1 stick) butter**

6 **stalks celery, sliced**

2 **onions, chopped**

2 **cans (4 ounces each) sliced mushrooms, drained**

¼ **cup plus 2 tablespoons all-purpose flour**

2 **cans (10¾ ounces each) condensed cream of celery soup, undiluted**

5 **to 6 ounces garlic cheese, cut into cubes**

2 **packages (10 ounces each) frozen broccoli spears**

French bread slices, bell pepper strips, cherry tomatoes

1. Melt butter in large skillet over medium heat. Add celery, onions and mushrooms; cook and stir until onions are translucent. Stir in flour; cook 2 to 3 minutes. Transfer to **CROCK-POT®** slow cooker.

2. Stir in soup, cheese and broccoli. Cover; cook on HIGH until cheese is melted, stirring every 15 minutes. Turn **CROCK-POT®** slow cooker to LOW. Cover; cook 2 to 4 hours or until ready to serve.

3. Serve warm with bread slices and assorted vegetables.

Makes about 6 cups

Prep Time: 10 to 15 minutes

Teriyaki Chicken Wings

- **3 to 4 pounds chicken wings**
- **¼ cup soy sauce**
- **¼ cup dry sherry**
- **¼ cup honey**
- **1 tablespoon hoisin sauce**
- **1 tablespoon orange juice**
- **2 cloves garlic, minced**
- **1 fresh red chile pepper, finely chopped* (optional)**

*Chile peppers can sting and irritate the skin, so wear rubber gloves when handling and do not touch your eyes.

1. Place wings in **CROCK-POT®** slow cooker. Combine remaining ingredients in medium bowl; pour over wings.

2. Cover; cook on LOW 3 to 3½ hours or on HIGH 1½ to 2 hours.

Makes 6 to 8 servings

Prep Time: 10 minutes
Cook Time: 3 to 3½ hours (LOW) or 1½ to 2 hours (HIGH)

Pepperoni Pizza Dip with Breadstick Dippers

- 1 jar or can (14 ounces) pizza sauce
- ¾ cup chopped turkey pepperoni
- 4 green onions, chopped
- 1 can (2 ¼ ounces) sliced black olives, drained
- ½ teaspoon dried oregano
- 1 cup (4 ounces) shredded mozzarella cheese
- 1 package (3 ounces) cream cheese, softened
  Breadstick Dippers (recipe follows)

1. Combine pizza sauce, pepperoni, green onions, olives and oregano in 2-quart **CROCK-POT®** slow cooker. Cover; cook on LOW 2 hours or on HIGH 1 to 1½ hours or until mixture is heated through.

2. Stir in mozzarella cheese and cream cheese until melted and well blended. Serve with warm Breadstick Dippers.

Makes 8 servings

Breadstick Dippers

- 1 package (8 ounces) refrigerated breadstick dough
- 2 teaspoons melted butter
- 2 teaspoons minced fresh Italian parsley

Bake breadsticks according to package directions. Brush with melted butter and sprinkle with parsley. Serve with warm dip.

Creamy Artichoke-Parmesan Dip

- **2 cans (14 ounces each) artichoke hearts, drained and chopped**
- **2 cups (8 ounces) shredded mozzarella cheese**
- **1½ cups grated Parmesan cheese**
- **1½ cups mayonnaise**
- **½ cup finely chopped onion**
- **½ teaspoon dried oregano**
- **¼ teaspoon garlic powder**
- **4 pita bread rounds, cut into wedges**
- **Assorted cut-up vegetables**

Place artichokes, mozzarella cheese, Parmesan cheese, mayonnaise, onion, oregano and garlic powder in 1½-quart or other small-sized **CROCK-POT®** slow cooker; mix well. Cover; cook on LOW 2 hours. Arrange pita bread wedges and vegetables on platter; serve with warm dip.

Makes about 4 cups

Tip: When adapting conventionally prepared recipes for your **CROCK-POT®** slow cooker, revise the amount of herbs and spices you use. For example, whole herbs and spices increase in flavor while ground spices tend to lose flavor during slow cooking. You can adjust the seasonings or add fresh herbs and spices just before serving the dish.

Bagna Cauda

- ¾ **cup olive oil**
- 6 **tablespoons butter, softened**
- 12 **anchovy fillets, drained**
- 6 **cloves garlic, peeled**
- ⅛ **teaspoon red pepper flakes**
  Assorted foods for dipping such as endive spears, cauliflower florets, cucumber spears, carrot sticks, zucchini spears, red bell pepper strips, sugar snap peas or crusty Italian or French bread slices

Place oil, butter, anchovies, garlic and red pepper flakes in food processor; process until smooth. Pour into 2½-quart or other small-sized **CROCK-POT®** slow cooker. Cover; cook on LOW 2 hours or until heated through. Serve with assorted dippers.

Makes 10 to 12 servings

Tip: Bagna cauda is a warm Italian dip similar to the more famous fondue. The name is derived from "bagno caldo," meaning "warm bath" in Italian. This dip should be kept warm while serving, just like you would fondue.

Bacon-Wrapped Fingerling Potatoes with Thyme

1 pound fingerling potatoes

2 tablespoons olive oil

1 tablespoon minced fresh thyme

½ teaspoon black pepper

¼ teaspoon paprika

½ pound bacon strips

¼ cup chicken broth

1. Toss potatoes with oil, thyme, pepper and paprika in large bowl.

2. Cut each bacon slice in half lengthwise; wrap half slice bacon tightly around each potato.

3. Heat large skillet over medium heat; add potatoes. Reduce heat to medium-low; cook until lightly browned and bacon has tightened around potatoes.

4. Place potatoes in **CROCK-POT®** slow cooker. Add broth. Cover; cook on HIGH 3 hours.

Makes 6 servings

Prep Time: 45 minutes
Cook Time: 3 hours (HIGH)

Tip: This appetizer can be made even more eye-catching with rare varieties of potatoes. Many interesting types of small potatoes can be found at farmers' markets. Purple potatoes, about the size of fingerling potatoes, can add some more color and pizazz to this dish.

Tuscan White Bean Soup

- **10 cups chicken broth**
- **1 package (16 ounces) dried Great Northern beans, rinsed and sorted**
- **1 can (about 14 ounces) diced tomatoes**
- **1 onion, chopped**
- **3 carrots, chopped**
- **6 ounces bacon, crisp-cooked and diced**
- **4 cloves garlic, minced**
- **1 fresh rosemary sprig *or* 1 teaspoon dried rosemary**
- **1 teaspoon black pepper**

1. Combine broth, beans, tomatoes, onion, carrots, bacon, garlic, rosemary sprig and pepper in **CROCK-POT®** slow cooker.

2. Cover; cook on LOW 8 hours. Remove and discard rosemary sprig before serving.

Makes 8 to 10 servings

Serving Suggestion: Place slices of toasted Italian bread in bottom of individual soup bowls. Drizzle with olive oil. Ladle soup over bread and serve.

Nana's Mini Meatball Soup

1	pound ground beef
1	pound ground pork
1½	cups finely grated Pecorino Romano or Parmesan cheese
1	cup Italian seasoned dry bread crumbs
2	eggs
1	bunch fresh Italian parsley
	Kosher salt and black pepper
3	quarts chicken broth
1	bunch escarole, coarsely chopped
½	(16-ounce) package ditalini pasta, cooked and drained

1. Combine beef, pork, cheese, bread crumbs, eggs, parsley, salt and pepper in large bowl until well blended. Shape into ¾-inch meatballs.

2. Add meatballs and broth to **CROCK-POT®** slow cooker. Cover; cook on LOW 9 hours or on HIGH 5 hours.

3. Add escarole; cook on LOW 15 minutes or until wilted. Stir in pasta just before serving.

Makes 8 servings

Tip: You may substitute spinach for escarole, if desired.

Lentil Soup with Ham and Bacon

- **8 ounces chopped bacon**
- **8 cups beef broth**
- **1½ pounds dried lentils, rinsed and sorted**
- **2 cups chopped ham**
- **1 cup chopped carrots**
- **¾ cup chopped celery**
- **¾ cup chopped tomatoes**
- **½ cup chopped onion**
- **2 teaspoons salt**
- **2 teaspoons black pepper**
- **½ teaspoon dried marjoram**

1. Heat skillet over medium heat. Add bacon; cook and stir until crisp. Transfer to **CROCK-POT®** slow cooker using slotted spoon.

2. Add broth, lentils, ham, carrots, celery, tomatoes, onion, salt, pepper and marjoram. Cover; cook on LOW 8 to 10 hours or on HIGH 6 to 8 hours or until lentils are tender.

Makes 8 servings

Cook Time: 8 to 10 hours (LOW) or 6 to 8 hours (HIGH)

Cauliflower Soup

2 heads cauliflower, cut into small florets

8 cups chicken broth

¾ cup chopped celery

¾ cup chopped onion

2 teaspoons salt

2 teaspoons black pepper

2 cups milk

1 teaspoon Worcestershire sauce

1. Combine cauliflower, broth, celery, onions, salt and pepper in **CROCK-POT®** slow cooker. Cover; cook on LOW 7 to 8 hours or on HIGH 3 to 4 hours.

2. Process soup until smooth using hand mixer or immersion blender. Add milk and Worcestershire sauce; process until blended. Cover; cook on HIGH 15 to 20 minutes or until heated through.

Makes 8 servings

Cook Time: 7 to 8 hours (LOW) or 3 to 4 hours (HIGH), plus 15 to 20 minutes (HIGH)

Beef Fajita Soup

- 1 **pound beef stew meat**
- 1 **can (about 15 ounces) pinto beans, rinsed and drained**
- 1 **can (about 15 ounces) black beans, rinsed and drained**
- 1 **can (about 14 ounces) diced tomatoes with roasted garlic**
- 1 **can (about 14 ounces) beef broth**
- 1½ **cups water**
- 1 **green bell pepper, thinly sliced**
- 1 **red bell pepper, thinly sliced**
- 1 **onion, thinly sliced**
- 2 **teaspoons ground cumin**
- 1 **teaspoon seasoned salt**
- 1 **teaspoon black pepper**

Combine beef, beans, tomatoes, broth, water, bell peppers, onion, cumin, salt and black pepper in **CROCK-POT®** slow cooker. Cover; cook on LOW 8 hours.

Makes 8 servings

Serving Suggestion: Serve topped with sour cream, shredded Monterey Jack or Cheddar cheese and chopped olives.

Chuck and Stout Soup

- **2 tablespoons olive oil**
- **3 pounds beef chuck roast, cut into 1-inch cubes**
- **Kosher salt and black pepper**
- **8 cups beef broth**
- **3 onions, thinly sliced**
- **3 stalks celery, diced**
- **6 carrots, diced**
- **4 cloves garlic, minced**
- **2 packages (10 ounces each) cremini mushrooms, thinly sliced**
- **1 package (about 1 ounce) dried porcini mushrooms, processed to a fine powder**
- **4 sprigs fresh thyme**
- **1 bottle (12 ounces) stout beer**
- **Fresh Italian parsley (optional)**

1. Heat oil in large skillet over medium-high heat. Season beef with salt and pepper. Working in batches, brown beef on all sides. Bring broth to a boil in large saucepan over high heat. Reduce heat to low; simmer until reduced by half.

2. Transfer beef to **CROCK-POT®** slow cooker. Add reduced broth and all remaining ingredients except parsley. Cover; cook on LOW 10 hours or on HIGH 6 hours. Garnish with parsley just before serving.

Makes 8 servings

Note: A coffee grinder works best for processing dried mushrooms, but a food processor or blender can also be used.

Savory Chicken and Oregano Chili

3 **cans (about 15 ounces each) Great Northern or cannellini beans, rinsed and drained**

3½ **cups chicken broth**

2 **cups chopped cooked chicken**

2 **red bell peppers, chopped**

1 **onion, chopped**

1 **can (4 ounces) diced mild green chiles, drained**

3 **cloves garlic, minced**

2 **teaspoons ground cumin**

1 **teaspoon salt**

1 **tablespoon minced fresh oregano**

1. Place beans, broth, chicken, bell peppers, onion, chiles, garlic, cumin and salt in **CROCK-POT®** slow cooker; mix well. Cover; cook on LOW 8 to 10 hours or on HIGH 4 to 5 hours.

2. Stir in oregano just before serving.

Makes 8 servings

Prep Time: 10 minutes
Cook Time: 8 to 10 hours (LOW) or 4 to 5 hours (HIGH)

Winter's Best Bean Soup

- 6 **ounces bacon, diced**
- 10 **cups chicken broth**
- 3 **cans (about 15 ounces each) Great Northern beans, rinsed and drained**
- 1 **can (about 14 ounces) diced tomatoes**
- 1 **onion, chopped**
- 1 **package (10 ounces) frozen sliced or diced carrots**
- 2 **teaspoons minced garlic**
- 1 **fresh rosemary sprig** *or* 1 **teaspoon dried rosemary**
- 1 **teaspoon black pepper**

1. Heat skillet over medium heat. Add bacon; cook and stir until crisp. Transfer to **CROCK-POT®** slow cooker using slotted spoon. Add broth, beans, tomatoes, onion, carrots, garlic, rosemary sprig and pepper.

2. Cover; cook on LOW 8 hours or until beans are tender. Remove rosemary sprig. Mince leaves and add to soup before serving.

Makes 8 to 10 servings

Serving Suggestion: Place slices of toasted Italian bread in bottom of individual soup bowls. Drizzle with olive oil. Pour soup over bread and serve.

Beef Chuck Chili

- ½ **cup plus 2 tablespoons olive oil, divided**
- 5 **pounds beef chuck roast, trimmed**
- 3 **cups minced onions**
- 4 **poblano peppers, seeded and diced***
- 2 **serrano peppers, seeded and diced***
- 2 **green bell peppers, seeded and diced**
- 3 **jalapeño peppers, seeded and diced****
- 2 **tablespoons minced garlic**
- 1 **can (28 ounces) crushed tomatoes, undrained**
- ½ **cup Mexican lager**
- ¼ **cup hot pepper sauce**
- 1 **tablespoon ground cumin**
- **Corn bread**

*Handle fresh chile peppers as directed for jalapeño peppers.

**Jalapeño peppers can sting and irritate the skin. Wear rubber gloves when handling peppers and do not touch your eyes.

1. Heat ½ cup oil in large skillet over medium-high heat. Add beef; sear on both sides. Transfer to **CROCK-POT®** slow cooker.

2. Heat remaining 2 tablespoons oil in same skillet over low heat. Add onions, peppers and garlic; cook and stir 7 minutes or until onions are tender. Transfer to **CROCK-POT®** slow cooker. Stir in tomatoes. Cover; cook on LOW 4 to 5 hours or until beef is fork-tender.

3. Remove beef from **CROCK-POT®** slow cooker; shred with two forks. Add lager, hot pepper sauce and cumin to cooking liquid. Return beef to cooking liquid; mix well. Serve over corn bread.

Makes 8 to 10 servings

Hearty Mushroom and Barley Soup

- **9** cups chicken broth
- **1** package (16 ounces) sliced mushrooms
- **1** onion, chopped
- **2** carrots, chopped
- **2** stalks celery, chopped
- **½** cup uncooked pearl barley
- **½** ounce dried porcini mushrooms
- **3** cloves garlic, minced
- **1** teaspoon salt
- **½** teaspoon dried thyme
- **½** teaspoon black pepper

Combine broth, sliced mushrooms, onion, carrots, celery, barley, dried mushrooms, garlic, salt, thyme and pepper in **CROCK-POT®** slow cooker. Cover; cook on LOW 4 to 6 hours.

Makes 8 to 10 servings

Variation: For even more flavor, try adding a beef or ham bone to the **CROCK-POT®** slow cooker with the rest of the ingredients.

Bring-Along Classics

Barbecue Roast Beef

2 pounds boneless cooked roast beef

1 bottle (12 ounces) barbecue sauce

1½ cups water

10 to 12 sandwich rolls, halved

1. Combine roast beef, barbecue sauce and water in **CROCK-POT®** slow cooker. Cover; cook on LOW 2 hours.

2. Remove beef from **CROCK-POT®** slow cooker; shred with two forks. Return beef to sauce; mix well. Serve on rolls.

Makes 10 to 12 servings

Prep Time: 5 minutes
Cook Time: 2 hours (LOW)

Tip: To save time, freeze leftovers as individual portions. Just reheat in a microwave for fast meals!

Shepherd's Pie

- 1 **pound ground beef**
- 1 **pound ground lamb**
- 1 **package (12 ounces) frozen chopped onions**
- 2 **teaspoons minced garlic**
- 1 **package (16 ounces) frozen peas and carrots**
- 1 **can (about 14 ounces) diced tomatoes, drained**
- 3 **tablespoons quick-cooking tapioca**
- 2 **teaspoons dried oregano**
- 1 **teaspoon salt**
- ½ **teaspoon black pepper**
- 2 **packages (24 ounces each) prepared mashed potatoes**

1. Brown beef and lamb in large nonstick skillet over medium-high heat, stirring to break up meat. Transfer to **CROCK-POT®** slow cooker using slotted spoon. Return skillet to heat and add onions and garlic. Cook and stir until onions are tender. Transfer to **CROCK-POT®** slow cooker.

2. Stir in peas and carrots, tomatoes, tapioca, oregano, salt and pepper. Cover; cook on LOW 7 to 8 hours.

3. Top with prepared mashed potatoes. Cover; cook on LOW 30 minutes or until potatoes are heated through.

Makes 6 servings

Chicken with Italian Sausage

10 ounces bulk mild or hot Italian sausage

6 boneless skinless chicken thighs, trimmed

1 can (about 15 ounces) white beans, rinsed and drained

1 can (about 15 ounces) red beans, rinsed and drained

1 cup chicken broth

1 onion, chopped

1 teaspoon black pepper

½ teaspoon salt

Chopped fresh parsley

1. Brown sausage in large skillet over medium-high heat, stirring to break up meat. Transfer to **CROCK-POT®** slow cooker using slotted spoon.

2. Add chicken, beans, broth, onion, pepper and salt to **CROCK-POT®** slow cooker. Cover; cook on LOW 5 to 6 hours.

3. Serve chicken with sausage and beans. Garnish with parsley.

Makes 6 servings

Suzie's Sloppy Joes

3 pounds ground beef

1 cup chopped onion

3 cloves garlic, minced

1¼ cups ketchup

1 cup chopped red bell pepper

¼ cup plus 1 tablespoon Worcestershire sauce

¼ cup packed dark brown sugar

3 tablespoons prepared mustard

3 tablespoons vinegar

2 teaspoons chili powder

Toasted hamburger buns

1. Brown beef, onion and garlic in large nonstick skillet over medium-high heat, stirring to break up meat. Drain fat.

2. Combine ketchup, bell pepper, Worcestershire sauce, brown sugar, mustard, vinegar and chili powder in **CROCK-POT®** slow cooker. Stir in beef mixture. Cover; cook on LOW 6 to 8 hours. Serve on buns.

Makes 8 servings

Prep Time: 15 to 20 minutes
Cook Time: 6 to 8 hours (LOW)

Slow Cooker Chicken Dinner

4 boneless skinless chicken breasts (about 1 pound)

1 can (10¾ ounces) condensed cream of chicken soup, undiluted

⅓ cup milk

1 package (6 ounces) stuffing mix

1⅔ cups water

1. Place chicken in **CROCK-POT®** slow cooker. Combine soup and milk in small bowl; pour over chicken.

2. Combine stuffing mix and water. Spoon stuffing over chicken. Cover; cook on LOW 6 to 8 hours.

Makes 4 servings

Prep Time: 5 minutes
Cook Time: 6 to 8 hours (LOW)

Fantastic Pot Roast

1 can (12 ounces) cola

1 bottle (10 ounces) chili sauce

2 cloves garlic (optional)

2½ pounds boneless beef chuck roast

Combine cola, chili sauce and garlic, if desired, in **CROCK-POT®** slow cooker. Add beef; turn to coat. Cover; cook on LOW 6 to 8 hours. Serve with sauce.

Makes 6 servings

Prep Time: 5 minutes
Cook Time: 6 to 8 hours (LOW)

Slow Cooker Chicken Dinner

Wild Rice with Fruit & Nuts

2 cups wild rice (or wild rice blend), rinsed*

½ cup dried cranberries

½ cup chopped raisins

½ cup chopped dried apricots

½ cup almond slivers, toasted**

5 to 6 cups chicken broth

1 cup orange juice

2 tablespoons butter, melted

1 teaspoon ground cumin

2 green onions, thinly sliced

2 to 3 tablespoons chopped fresh parsley

Salt and black pepper

*Do not use parboiled rice or a blend containing parboiled rice.
**To toast almonds, spread in single layer in small heavy skillet. Cook over medium heat 1 to 2 minutes, stirring frequently, until lightly browned. Remove from skillet immediately. Cool before using.

1. Combine wild rice, cranberries, raisins, apricots and almonds in **CROCK-POT®** slow cooker.

2. Combine broth, orange juice, butter and cumin in medium bowl. Pour mixture over rice and stir to mix.

3. Cover; cook on LOW 7 hours or on HIGH 2½ to 3 hours. Stir once, adding more hot broth if necessary.

4. When rice is tender, stir in green onions and parsley. Season with salt and pepper. Cover; cook on LOW 10 minutes.

Makes 6 to 8 servings

Corned Beef and Cabbage

- 12 new red potatoes, quartered
- 4 carrots, sliced
- 1 corned beef brisket (about 4 pounds)
- 2 onions, sliced
- 3 whole bay leaves
- 8 whole black peppercorns
- 1 head cabbage, cut into wedges

1. Place potatoes and carrots in bottom of **CROCK-POT®** slow cooker. Add brisket, onions, bay leaves and peppercorns. Add enough water to cover brisket. Cover; cook on LOW 4 to 5 hours or on HIGH 2 to 2½ hours.

2. Add cabbage. Cover; cook on LOW 4 to 5 hours or on HIGH 2 to 2½ hours. Slice brisket against the grain; serve with vegetables.

Makes 6 to 8 servings

Prep Time: 10 minutes
Cook Time: 8 to 10 hours (LOW) or 4 to 5 hours (HIGH)

Caribbean Sweet Potato and Bean Stew

- **2 sweet potatoes (about 1 pound), cut into 1-inch cubes**
- **2 cups frozen cut green beans**
- **1 can (about 15 ounces) black beans, rinsed and drained**
- **1 can (about 14 ounces) vegetable broth**
- **1 onion, sliced**
- **2 teaspoons Caribbean jerk seasoning**
- **½ teaspoon dried thyme**
- **¼ teaspoon salt**
- **¼ teaspoon ground cinnamon**
- **⅓ cup slivered almonds, toasted***

*To toast almonds, spread in single layer on baking sheet. Bake in preheated 350°F oven 8 to 10 minutes or until golden brown, stirring frequently.

Combine sweet potatoes, green beans, black beans, broth, onion, seasoning, thyme, salt and cinnamon in **CROCK-POT®** slow cooker. Cover; cook on LOW 5 to 6 hours or until vegetables are tender. Serve with almonds.

Makes 4 servings

Hearty Cassoulet

- 1 tablespoon olive oil
- 1 onion, finely chopped
- 4 boneless skinless chicken thighs, chopped
- ¼ pound smoked turkey sausage, finely chopped
- 3 cloves garlic, minced
- 1 teaspoon dried thyme
- ½ teaspoon black pepper
- 4 tablespoons tomato paste
- 2 tablespoons water
- 3 cans (about 15 ounces each) Great Northern beans, rinsed and drained
- ½ cup plain dry bread crumbs
- 3 tablespoons minced fresh parsley

1. Heat oil in large skillet over medium heat. Add onion; cook and stir 5 minutes or until tender. Add chicken, sausage, garlic, thyme and pepper; cook and stir 5 minutes or until chicken and sausage are browned.

2. Remove skillet from heat; stir in tomato paste and water until blended. Transfer to **CROCK-POT®** slow cooker. Stir in beans. Cover; cook on LOW 4 to 4½ hours.

3. Before serving, combine bread crumbs and parsley in small bowl. Sprinkle over top of cassoulet.

Makes 6 servings

Tip: When preparing ingredients for the **CROCK-POT®** slow cooker, cut into uniform pieces so that everything cooks evenly.

Korean Barbecue Beef

4 **to 4½ pounds beef short ribs**

¼ **cup chopped green onions**

¼ **cup tamari or soy sauce**

¼ **cup beef broth or water**

1 **tablespoon packed brown sugar**

2 **teaspoons minced fresh ginger**

2 **teaspoons minced garlic**

½ **teaspoon black pepper**

2 **teaspoons dark sesame oil**

Hot cooked rice

2 **teaspoons sesame seeds, toasted***

*To toast sesame seeds, spread in small skillet. Shake skillet over medium-low heat 2 minutes or until seeds begin to pop and turn golden brown.

1. Place ribs in **CROCK-POT®** slow cooker. Combine green onions, tamari, broth, brown sugar, ginger, garlic and pepper in medium bowl; pour over ribs. Cover; cook on LOW 7 to 8 hours or until ribs are fork-tender.

2. Remove ribs from cooking liquid. Cool slightly. Trim excess fat and discard. Cut rib meat into bite-size pieces, discarding bones.

3. Let cooking liquid stand 5 minutes to allow fat to rise. Skim off fat and discard. Stir sesame oil into cooking liquid.

4. Return beef to cooking liquid in **CROCK-POT®** slow cooker. Cover; cook on LOW 15 to 30 minutes or until heated through. Serve over rice; sprinkle with sesame seeds.

Makes 6 servings

Jamaica-Me-Crazy Chicken Tropicale

- 2 sweet potatoes, cut into 2-inch pieces
- 1 can (20 ounces) pineapple tidbits in pineapple juice, drained and juice reserved
- 1 can (8 ounces) water chestnuts, drained and sliced
- 1 cup golden raisins
- 4 boneless skinless chicken breasts
- 4 teaspoons Caribbean jerk seasoning
- ¼ cup dried onion flakes
- 3 tablespoons grated fresh ginger
- 2 tablespoons Worcestershire sauce
- 1 tablespoon grated lime peel
- 1 teaspoon whole cumin seeds, slightly crushed
- Hot cooked rice (optional)

1. Place sweet potatoes in **CROCK-POT®** slow cooker. Add pineapple tidbits, water chestnuts and raisins; mix well. Sprinkle chicken with seasoning. Place chicken on top of sweet potato mixture.

2. Combine reserved pineapple juice, onion flakes, ginger, Worcestershire sauce, lime peel and cumin seeds in small bowl; pour over chicken. Cover; cook on LOW 7 to 9 hours or on HIGH 3 to 4 hours or until chicken and sweet potatoes are fork-tender. Serve with rice, if desired.

Makes 4 servings

Prep Time: 10 minutes
Cook Time: 7 to 9 hours (LOW) or 3 to 4 hours (HIGH)

Cuban Black Beans and Rice

- 3¾ cups chicken broth
- 1½ cups uncooked brown rice
- 1 onion, chopped
- 1 jalapeño pepper, seeded and chopped*
- 3 cloves garlic, minced
- 2 teaspoons ground cumin
- 1 teaspoon salt
- 2 cans (about 15 ounces each) black beans, rinsed and drained
- 1 tablespoon lime juice
- Sour cream (optional)
- Chopped green onions (optional)

*Jalapeño peppers can sting and irritate the skin, so wear rubber gloves when handling peppers and do not touch your eyes.

1. Place broth, rice, onion, jalapeño pepper, garlic, cumin and salt in **CROCK-POT®** slow cooker; mix well. Cover; cook on LOW 7½ hours or until rice is tender.

2. Stir in beans and lime juice. Cover; cook on LOW 15 to 20 minutes or until heated through. Garnish with sour cream and green onions.

Makes 4 to 6 servings

Chinese Cashew Chicken

1 can (16 ounces) bean sprouts, drained

2 cups sliced cooked chicken

1 can (10¾ ounces) condensed cream of mushroom soup, undiluted

1 cup sliced celery

½ cup chopped green onions

1 can (4 ounces) sliced mushrooms, drained

3 tablespoons butter

1 tablespoon soy sauce

1 cup whole cashews

Hot cooked rice

1. Combine bean sprouts, chicken, soup, celery, green onions, mushrooms, butter and soy sauce in **CROCK-POT®** slow cooker. Cover; cook on LOW 4 to 6 hours or on HIGH 2 to 3 hours.

2. Stir in cashews just before serving. Serve over rice.

Makes 4 servings

Tip: For easier preparation, cut up the ingredients for this **CROCK-POT®** slow cooker recipe the night before. Don't place the **CROCK-POT®** stoneware in the refrigerator. Instead, wrap and refrigerate the chicken and vegetables separately.

Ginger Beef with Peppers and Mushrooms

- 1½ **pounds beef top round steak, cut into ¾-inch cubes**
- 24 **baby carrots**
- 1 **red bell pepper, chopped**
- 1 **green bell pepper, chopped**
- 1 **onion, chopped**
- 1 **package (8 ounces) mushrooms, cut in halves**
- 1 **cup reduced-sodium beef broth**
- ½ **cup hoisin sauce**
- ¼ **cup quick-cooking tapioca**
- 2 **tablespoons grated fresh ginger**
  Hot cooked rice (optional)

Combine beef, carrots, bell peppers, onion, mushrooms, broth, hoisin sauce, tapioca and ginger in **CROCK-POT®** slow cooker. Cover; cook on LOW 8 to 9 hours. Serve over rice, if desired.

Makes 6 servings

Tip: Boneless beef top round steak can also sometimes be found in the meat section packaged as London Broil. Both are the same cut of beef, however London Broil is a particularly thick cut of top round.

Ham and Cheese Pasta Bake

- 6 **cups water**
- 2 **teaspoons salt**
- 12 **ounces uncooked rigatoni pasta**
- 1 **ham steak, cubed**
- 1 **container (10 ounces) refrigerated light Alfredo sauce**
- 2 **cups (8 ounces) shredded mozzarella cheese, divided**
- 2 **cups half-and-half, warmed**
- 1 **tablespoon cornstarch**

1. Bring water to a boil in medium saucepan. Stir in salt. Add pasta; boil 7 minutes. Drain pasta; transfer to **CROCK-POT®** slow cooker.

2. Stir in ham, Alfredo sauce and 1 cup cheese. Whisk half-and-half into cornstarch in small bowl until smooth; pour over pasta. Sprinkle with remaining cheese. Cover; cook on LOW 3½ to 4 hours or until pasta is tender and excess liquid is absorbed.

Makes 6 servings

Prep Time: 15 minutes
Cook Time: 3½ to 4 hours (LOW)

Thai Chili Chicken and Noodles

2 **teaspoons olive oil**

1½ **pounds boneless skinless chicken breasts, cut into thin strips**

1 **bottle (about 10 ounces) Asian-style sweet chili sauce***

3 **tablespoons creamy peanut butter**

3 **cloves garlic, minced**

1 **can (about 14 ounces) chicken broth**

1 **package (8 ounces) uncooked vermicelli noodles**

1 **cup shredded cabbage and carrot mix**

Bean sprouts (optional)

Chopped fresh cilantro (optional)

Chopped roasted peanuts (optional)

*Asian-style sweet chili sauce can be found in the ethnic foods aisle of many supermarkets.

1. Heat oil in large nonstick skillet over medium-high heat. Working in batches, brown chicken on all sides. Transfer to **CROCK-POT®** slow cooker.

2. Combine sweet chili sauce, peanut butter and garlic in small bowl; pour over chicken, stirring to coat. Stir in broth. Cover; cook on LOW 2 hours.

3. Add noodles and cabbage and carrot mix; cover and cook on LOW 30 minutes or until noodles and vegetables are tender. Garnish with bean sprouts, cilantro and peanuts.

Makes 4 to 6 servings

Ziti Ratatouille

1   **large eggplant, peeled and cut into ½-inch cubes (about 1½ pounds)**

2   **zucchini, cut into ½-inch cubes**

1   **green or red bell pepper, cut into ½-inch pieces**

1   **onion, chopped**

4   **cloves garlic, minced**

1   **jar (about 24 ounces) marinara sauce**

2   **cans (about 14 ounces each) diced tomatoes with garlic and onions**

1   **package (8 ounces) uncooked ziti pasta**

1   **can (6 ounces) pitted black olives, drained**

Lemon juice (optional)

Shaved Parmesan cheese (optional)

1. Layer eggplant, zucchini, bell pepper, onion, garlic, marinara sauce and tomatoes in **CROCK-POT®** slow cooker. Cover; cook on LOW 4½ hours.

2. Stir in pasta and olives; cover and cook on LOW 25 minutes or until pasta is tender. Drizzle with lemon juice and sprinkle with cheese, if desired.

Makes 6 to 8 servings

Southwestern Mac and Cheese

- 1 **package (8 ounces) uncooked elbow macaroni**
- 1 **can (about 14 ounces) diced tomatoes with green peppers and onions**
- 1 **can (10 ounces) diced tomatoes with green chiles**
- 1½ **cups salsa**
- 3 **cups (12 ounces) shredded Mexican cheese blend, divided**

1. Coat **CROCK-POT®** slow cooker with nonstick cooking spray. Layer macaroni, tomatoes, salsa and 2 cups cheese in **CROCK-POT®** slow cooker. Cover; cook on LOW 3 hours 45 minutes or until macaroni is tender.

2. Sprinkle remaining 1 cup cheese over macaroni. Cover; cook on LOW 15 minutes or until cheese is melted.

Makes 6 servings

Prep Time: 5 minutes
Cook Time: 4 hours (LOW)

Turkey Paprikash

2 tablespoons all-purpose flour

¼ teaspoon *each* salt, black pepper and sweet paprika

⅛ teaspoon red pepper flakes

1 pound turkey breast, cut into bite-size pieces

2 tablespoons olive oil

1 onion, chopped

1 clove garlic, minced

1 can (about 14 ounces) diced tomatoes

12 ounces uncooked wide egg noodles

¼ cup sour cream

Sliced pimiento-stuffed green olives

1. Combine flour, salt, black pepper, paprika and red pepper flakes in large resealable food storage bag. Add turkey; shake to coat. Heat oil in large skillet over medium-high heat. Add turkey in single layer; brown on all sides. Arrange turkey in single layer in **CROCK-POT®** slow cooker.

2. Add onion and garlic to skillet; cook and stir 2 minutes or until onion is browned. Transfer to **CROCK-POT®** slow cooker. Stir in tomatoes. Cover; cook on LOW 1 to 2 hours or until turkey is tender.

3. Meanwhile, cook noodles until tender. Drain and place in large shallow bowl. Spoon turkey and sauce over noodles. Top with sour cream and olives.

Makes 4 servings

Prep Time: 15 minutes

Macaroni and Cheese

- **6 cups cooked elbow macaroni**
- **2 tablespoons butter**
- **6 cups (24 ounces) shredded Cheddar cheese**
- **4 cups evaporated milk**
- **2 teaspoons salt**
- **½ teaspoon black pepper**

Toss macaroni with butter in large bowl. Stir in cheese, evaporated milk, salt and pepper. Transfer to **CROCK-POT®** slow cooker. Cover; cook on HIGH 2 to 3 hours.

Makes 6 to 8 servings

Prep Time: 10 to 15 minutes
Cook Time: 2 to 3 hours (HIGH)

Tip: Make this mac 'n' cheese recipe more fun by adding some tasty mix-ins. Diced green or red bell pepper, peas, hot dog slices, chopped tomato, browned ground beef or chopped onion are all great options. Be creative!

Roast Chicken with Peas, Prosciutto and Cream

1 whole chicken (about 2½ pounds), cut up
  Salt and black pepper
5 ounces prosciutto, diced
1 white onion, finely chopped
½ cup dry white wine
1 package (10 ounces) frozen peas
½ cup whipping cream
2 tablespoons water
1½ tablespoons cornstarch
4 cups farfalle pasta, cooked and drained

1. Season chicken with salt and pepper. Combine chicken, prosciutto, onion and wine in **CROCK-POT®** slow cooker. Cover; cook on LOW 8 to 10 hours or on HIGH 3½ to 4 hours.

2. During last 30 minutes of cooking, add frozen peas and cream to cooking liquid.

3. Remove chicken when cooked through. Carve into slices, discarding bones. Transfer chicken to warmed platter.

4. Stir water into cornstarch in small bowl until smooth. Stir into cooking liquid in **CROCK-POT®** slow cooker. Cover; cook on HIGH 10 to 15 minutes or until thickened.

5. Toss chicken with pasta and sauce.

Makes 6 servings

Cook Time: 8 to 10 hours (LOW) or 3½ to 4 hours (HIGH), plus 10 to 15 minutes (HIGH)

Cream Cheese Chicken with Broccoli

- **4** pounds boneless skinless chicken breasts, cut into ½-inch pieces
- **1** tablespoon olive oil
- **1** package (1 ounce) Italian salad dressing mix
   Nonstick cooking spray
- **2** cups (about 8 ounces) sliced mushrooms
- **1** cup chopped onion
- **1** can (10¾ ounces) condensed cream of chicken soup, undiluted
- **1** bag (10 ounces) frozen broccoli florets, thawed
- **1** package (8 ounces) cream cheese, cubed
- **¼** cup dry sherry
   Hot cooked pasta

1. Toss chicken with oil in large bowl. Sprinkle with salad dressing mix. Transfer to **CROCK-POT®** slow cooker. Cover; cook on LOW 3 hours.

2. Coat large skillet with cooking spray; heat over medium heat. Add mushrooms and onion; cook 5 minutes or until onion is tender, stirring occasionally.

3. Add soup, broccoli, cream cheese and sherry to skillet; cook and stir until heated through. Transfer to **CROCK-POT®** slow cooker. Cover; cook on LOW 1 hour. Serve chicken and sauce over pasta.

Makes 10 to 12 servings

Prep Time: 20 minutes
Cook Time: 4 hours (LOW)

Index